Did You K...

SURREY

A MISCELLANY

Compiled by Julia Skinner

With particular reference to the work of Keith Howell,
Hazelle Jackson, Helen Livingston and David Rose

THE FRANCIS FRITH COLLECTION

www.francisfrith.com

First published in the United Kingdom in 2010 by The Francis Frith Collection®

This edition published exclusively for Bradwell Books in 2013
For trade enquiries see: www.bradwellbooks.com or tel: 0800 834 920
ISBN 978-1-84589-543-3

Text and Design copyright The Francis Frith Collection®
Photographs copyright The Francis Frith Collection® except where indicated.

The Frith® photographs and the Frith® logo are reproduced under licence from
Heritage Photographic Resources Ltd, the owners of the Frith® archive and trademarks.
'The Francis Frith Collection', 'Francis Frith' and 'Frith' are registered trademarks of
Heritage Photographic Resources Ltd.

British Library Cataloguing in Publication Data

Did You Know? Surrey - A Miscellany
Compiled by Julia Skinner
With particular reference to the work of Keith Howell, Hazelle Jackson,
Helen Livingston and David Rose

The Francis Frith Collection
6, Oakley Business Park,
Wylye Road, Dinton, Wiltshire SP3 5EU
Tel: +44 (0) 1722 716 376
Email: info@francisfrith.co.uk
www.francisfrith.com

www.francisfrith.com

Printed and bound in Malaysia
Contains material sourced from responsibly managed forests

Front Cover: **FRIMLEY GREEN, OLD COTTAGE 1906** 54907p
Frontispiece: **MERROW, THE FORGE 1913** 65231v

The colour-tinting is for illustrative purposes only, and is not intended to be historically accurate

CONTENTS

INTRODUCTION

'This county of Surrey presents to the eye of the traveller a greater contrast than any other county of England. It has some of the very best and some of the worst lands…'

William Cobbett, from 'Rural Rides', published in 1830.

Surrey's beautiful landscape and picturesque towns and villages have been praised and loved for generations. In the 19th century many artists and writers flocked there to live and work in the peaceful countryside, and in those days Surrey certainly seemed a world away from London. Yet, for centuries, this most loved of the Home Counties has been within London's sphere. In recent years, many of the quaint 'old fashioned' aspects of the county that were so beloved of Victorian writers, artists and photographers have been crowded out. Surrey today is frequently considered a suburban county, a neat garden-and-parkland setting for houses of the wealthy, rather than real countryside. This is scarcely fair: Surrey is still primarily a land of working farms – but it is true that London has been a greedy neighbour. The 1889 London Government Act that created the new county of London captured part of Surrey and annexed the south bank of the River Thames – the bank still lovingly referred to by those who ply the river as 'the Surrey side'. Further incursions took place in 1965 and again in 1974, abolishing the old county of Middlesex (except as a postal district!) so that Staines, on the north bank of the Thames, became a Surrey town. Today Surrey has lost much of her traditional northern boundary along the Thames, but it still lays claim to sufficient of England's 'Royal River' through Staines and Chertsey, Walton and Weybridge, for this old watery highway to be an integral part of the county.

That Surrey retains a rural aspect is largely owing to the 'Green Belt' policy, which checks the physical expansion of London, and to the continued efforts of those who wish to preserve the landscape. That

HINDHEAD, THE ROYAL HUTS HOTEL 1909 61434

landscape is extremely varied, and therein lies much of the county's magic. The 'Surrey Hills' is an affectionate nickname, including the uplands of the greensand country and the rolling chalklands of the North Downs. Here are such renowned beauty spots as Leith Hill and Box Hill, beloved alike by generations of picnickers and walkers. Rivers have cut deep vales through the high chalkland. This is good farming country, under the plough and grazed by herds and flocks for generations, and the short, sweet turf of the North Downs has long been known for producing splendid sheep. North-west Surrey is of quite a different aspect, an upland region of sandy heaths and clumps of pines. Bagshot Heath in days gone by was the haunt of highwaymen, and now the whole area is given over to the army, which moved into north-west Surrey during Victorian times, taking over the heathland that was unprofitable to the farmer and, at that time, but sparsely populated. The high heaths continue into the south-west around Hindhead and Haslemere, where holidaymakers flock to gaze at the scenic valley of the Devil's Punchbowl. To the south-east, where it borders Sussex and Kent, Surrey lies in the clay Weald, that great expanse which glimmers into the distance in the views from the Surrey Hills.

3

SURREY DIALECT
WORDS AND PHRASES

'Horny bug' – a stag beetle.

'Bodger' – a stick or tool used to make a hole in the ground for planting seeds.

'Vairn' – fern.

'Apern' – apron.

'Chart' – is both a place name around Dorking and also a dialect word of Surrey and Kent. It comes from the Anglo-Saxon word 'ceart', meaning a rough common overgrown with gorse or bracken.

'Shick-shack' – a name for oak-apples in Surrey. 'Shick-Shack Day' was the Surrey name for Oak-Apple Day (29th May), which used to be a public holiday to celebrate the restoration of the monarchy in 1660. It was named after the oak tree in which Charles II hid from his pursuers whilst fleeing from the battle of Worcester in 1651.

The phrase **'using Ockham's razor'** (sometimes spelled Occam's) comes from the Surrey town of Ockham, between Dorking and Woking. William of Ockham (1270-1347) was a philosopher, theologian and Franciscan friar who developed the theory known as **'Ockham's Razor'**. Ockham's view was that when there are several competing theories to explain a phenomenon, the simpler theory is usually the most likely. The 'razor' of the name of the theory alludes to the idea of something cutting away unnecessary assumptions.

HAUNTED SURREY

There are many ghost stories around Surrey. Here are just a few:

The bridge over the River Mole at Cobham is reputed to be haunted by the weeping ghost of Queen Matilda, the first wife of Henry I (1100-1135); she is mourning the death of one of her handmaidens, who was drowned in the river near this spot.

Shepperton is said to be haunted by the headless phantom of a monk from Chertsey Abbey who broke his vows and ran off to live with a woman on a farm. He was pursued and beheaded for his sin, and his ghost roams the area where he lived with his lover, now covered with housing.

The old motor-racing circuit at Brooklands, near Weybridge, was the first purpose-built motorsport racing circuit in the world. The ghost of Percy Lambert, an early racing motorist who was killed there in 1913, is said to haunt the area. Night-workers at an aircraft factory built on the spot on the Railway Straight where Lambert met his death reported seeing a helmeted figure in overalls, which disappeared through a solid wall.

Pippbrook House at Dorking, which now houses the main library, is one of the town's best known haunted buildings. A ghostly butler is said to look out of one of the windows, and a phantom lady dressed in a long grey gown has been seen descending the stairs.

Box Hill is said to be haunted by a phantom horse rider; it was mentioned in a poem by Robert Louis Stevenson, who knew the area from staying at the Burford Bridge Hotel.

The Angel Hotel in Guildford is reputedly haunted by a ghostly man with a moustache dressed in an old-fashioned military uniform; in 1970 he appeared in a mirror in one of the bedrooms, looking back at two guests at the hotel.

SURREY MISCELLANY

Saxons and Jutes began settling in the Surrey area from the late fifth century. The name of Surrey comes from Anglo-Saxon etymology that probably means either 'the south ridge', alluding to the Surrey Hills, or 'the south region'.

In the Middle Ages particularly devout people would sometimes shut themselves into small cells for contemplation away from worldly life. The church of St James at Shere is famous for its 14th-century anchoress, or female hermit, Christine, the local carpenter's daughter, who was walled up in a cell against the wall of the church. After three years of holy imprisonment, Christine found it too much and left her cell in 1332. This was an unprecedented thing to do, for an anchoress was supposed to stay incarcerated until death, and Christine later returned to be walled up again and remained there for the rest of her life. The remains of her cell are outside the north wall of the chancel of the church.

MILFORD, FARMING c1955 M76060

BAGSHOT, THE BRIDGE HOUSE, HIGH STREET 1901 46844x

Bagshot was an important staging post on the old Portsmouth Road in the days of coaching travel. Bagshot Heath was a notorious haunt of highwaymen in the past, including William Davis, who worked a farm on the heath in the 17th century but for over 40 years also had a secret career of highway robbery. He was nicknamed the 'Golden Farmer' because he paid his debts in gold, most of which was robbed from travellers. The Jolly Farmer roundabout at Camberley is named after the building there that used to be the Jolly Farmer Inn but was originally called the Golden Farmer Inn, after William Davis. Beside the A30 near the roundabout is a stone on which a plaque reads: 'SITE OF THE BASING STONE AND LEGEND OF THE WHITE HART'. The original Basing Stone has now gone, but marked the spot where Richard II (1377-1399) was attacked by a wounded stag whilst hunting in the area and was saved by a white hart that came between them. In gratitude the king caused four hostelries with the sign of the White Hart to be erected in the region at Bagshot, Chobham, Frimley and Pirbright.

CAMBERLEY, HIGH STREET 1925 78125

Until the 19th century, Frimley was the largest settlement in the Blackwater Valley. Development of Camberley did not start until the Royal Military College's Senior Department was moved to the Sandhurst estate, just over the county border in Berkshire, in the 1820s; it was later renamed the Military Staff College, and Camberley grew up at its gates. Camberley was originally called 'Cambridge Town', but the name was changed to Camberley in 1877 to avoid confusion with the university town. During the 19th and 20th centuries, Camberley's growth engulfed the earlier military settlement at 'York Town' to the west, that had grown up when the army moved there from Marlow in 1812.

A landmark of Camberley is the concrete elephant on the A30 near The Meadows roundabout. It was designed in 1963 for a float in London's Lord Mayor's Show for the city builders Trollope & Colls. All but the ears of the elephant was made from standard concrete pipes, and it was constructed at the firm's Camberley pipeworks. After the Lord Mayor's Show it was put up over the entrance to the works, and is still there today.

The first British attempt to improve a river for navigation took place in Surrey in 1653 when Sir Richard Weston of Sutton Place made the River Wey navigable from Guildford to the Thames, so that Wealden oak could be transported downstream. In 1760 the navigation was extended upstream to Godalming, and the canal also shipped meal and corn as well as paper and gunpowder made in Surrey. The Basingstoke Canal, with its flight of 14 locks at Deepcut, was completed in 1794 and linked the Wey and Godalming Navigation with Basingstoke. Deepcut, known for its army camp, is named after the long, deep cutting that carries the canal across the high heathland of west Surrey. The Basingstoke Canal Navigation Company became bankrupt in 1866 and the canal fell into disrepair, but it was restored in the 1990s by the Surrey and Hampshire Canal Society.

DEEPCUT CAMP, GUNNERS AT WORK 1906 55053

Farnham is Surrey's most westerly town. During the 18th and 19th centuries hops were of prime importance to Farnham, which had five breweries and more inns than any other town in Surrey. Hop gardens once covered the western side of Castle Street and extended as far as the back gardens of houses in West Street. The hostelry known as the Hop Blossom at Long Garden Walk in the town centre is a reminder of this time. Farnham is renowned for its Georgian architecture, and The Museum of Farnham in West Street is housed in a fine Grade I listed Georgian townhouse, built in 1718 by a wealthy hop merchant, that is an outstanding example of Georgian architecture, with what has been described as 'one of the finest cut brick facades in the country'.

FARNHAM, THE BOROUGH 1913 65926

Photograph 65926 (opposite) shows The Borough in central Farnham in 1913. The old Victorian town hall is seen on the corner of Castle Street; this building was replaced in the 1930s by a neo-Gothic building designed by Harold Faulkner for the landowner Mr Borelli, who aimed to return architectural harmony to the town.

In the 19th and 20th centuries Farnham became famous for its pottery, known as Farnham Greenware, and particularly for its unusual 'owl jugs', in the shape of the bird.

One of Farnham's most famous sons, William Cobbett was born in the inn then called the Jolly Farmer in Bridge Square in the town in 1763 – it was later renamed the William Cobbett in his honour. William Cobbett was a radical politician, a prolific writer and a great humanist who railed in his writings against the many social injustices he saw around him. He is famous for his 'Rural Rides', an account of a series of horseback journeys that he made across southern England between 1821 and 1826, which provide a fascinating account of country life and landscapes at this period.

Farnham Castle was formerly the seat of the Bishop of Winchester, and later became the seat of the Bishop of Guildford. Downing Street in Farnham is so named because monks from nearby Waverley Abbey who had been visiting their bishop at Farnham Castle would take the street 'down' from the town and back to their home. Waverley Abbey was founded in 1128 and was the first house of Cistercians in England. It was dissolved by Henry VIII in 1536 and is now a ruin.

Inside Frensham's parish church of St Mary is what was traditionally claimed to be a witch's cauldron used by Mother Ludlam, who lived in a cave near Waverley Abbey in the Middle Ages. However, it is more likely that the giant cauldron is either a relic from the kitchen of Waverley Abbey, or that it was used in the past for brewing the 'church ale' drunk at parish festivals.

GUILDFORD, THE CASTLE 1895 35064

The ruinous 12th-century keep built of Bargate stone from Godalming is all that now remains of Guildford's once-great castle. It was essentially a 'pleasaunce', a place for relaxation and pleasure, and was a particular favourite of Henry III (1216-1272) who visited it frequently and made many improvements to the building. After the death of Henry III the castle fell into decline and became a prison. In 1885 Guildford Corporation bought part of the complex, including the keep and the moat, and developed the grounds as a pleasure garden.

Until the 17th century, Guildford's main industry was the manufacture of 'Guildford blue', the cloth made from the wool of local sheep. The wool was spun in cottages in the town and dyed blue with woad, which was grown locally. Racks Close in Guildford, on the edge of the castle grounds, got its name because here stood the racks on which newly dyed wool was spread to dry.

The name of the George Abbot public house in Guildford commemorates the son of a local cloth worker, born in Guildford in 1562, who served as Archbishop of Canterbury from 1611 until his death in 1633. In 1619 Archbishop Abbot founded his Hospital of the Blessed Trinity in the town, an almshouse to provide accommodation for twenty elderly residents of Guildford. The Hospital still discharges its original function, through the conditions of entry have been modified. Abbot's Hospital is one of Guildford's most beautiful buildings and one of the best examples of Tudor-style brickwork in the country. Archbishop Abbot's elaborate tomb – a Jacobean fantasy of skulls and books, with the archbishop portrayed life-size in marble – is in Holy Trinity Church in the High Street, opposite the Hospital.

GUILDFORD, ABBOT'S HOSPITAL 1903 50879

GUILDFORD, HIGH STREET AND THE GUILDHALL 1923 73381

A famous landmark of Guildford's High Street is the Aylward clock of 1683, jutting out from the Elizabethan Guildhall. The story goes that in the late 17th century a clockmaker by the name of John Aylward came to Guildford and tried to establish a shop in the town, but the Guild Merchant refused him permission. Accordingly, he set up shop on the Mount – just outside the town limits – and made the handsome clock for the Guildhall that is now the dominant feature on the High Street. In gratitude the Guild Merchant made him a member, and he was able to open a shop in the town.

The modern Cathedral of the Holy Spirit at Guildford was begun in 1936 and finally completed in 1966, built of bricks made from clay dug out of Stag Hill on which it stands. Its consecration took place in 1961 in the presence of Queen Elizabeth II, who was offered the spice cake that all reigning monarchs are traditionally presented with when visiting Guildford.

In 1895 John and Raymond Dennis arrived in Guildford and set up in business. Bicycles were their main trade at first, but they had turned to building motorised vehicles before the turn of the century. The Dennis brothers produced their motor vehicles at what is now known as Rodboro Buildings in Bridge Street, erected in 1905, which is the oldest surviving car factory in Britain – twenty years before Henry Ford experimented with the conveyor-belt production of motor vehicles, in Guildford the Dennis brothers had perfected such a system. The business was so successful that in 1917 the brothers had to move elsewhere and the Rodboro Boot and Shoe Company bought the premises and gave it their name. It is now used as a pub. The Dennis company made a wide range of motor vehicles, but the name is particularly associated with fire-engines.

In medieval times Godalming prospered from the production of woollen cloth, but in later centuries other important industries developed, including the quarrying of the local sandstone (called 'Bargate') and leather tanning. It was one of the leather mills that gave Godalming a claim to international fame – in 1811 a generator was installed in the Pullman's leather mill to provide electricity to light the mill and to power street lighting, and even house lighting, in Godalming itself. This made Godalming the first place in the world to have a public electricity supply, three weeks ahead of Chesterfield in Derbyshire.

The manor house at Westbrook at Godalming, now the Meath Epilepsy Trust care home, was once the home of the Oglethorpe family. A famous member of the family was General James Oglethorpe, who became MP for Haselemere in 1722. He was a noted philanthropist and social reformer, and was instrumental in getting Parliament to initiate reforms to the prison system. He was later a founding father of the colony of Georgia in the USA, which he originally envisaged as somewhere for Britain's 'worthy poor', insolvent people released from debtor's prison and oppressed Protestants from the Continent to be able to move to and make a new start.

GODALMING
THE MARKET HOUSE
1903 49198

Godalming's distinctive Georgian market house in the centre of town is known locally as 'The Pepperpot'. The ground floor was sometimes used as a market and the upstairs room served as a council meeting chamber until the council offices were built in Bridge Street in 1908.

In 1786 the Red Lion Inn at Thursley was a final stopping place for an unknown sailor who was subsequently robbed and murdered by his three drinking companions on the heights above the village. The villains were captured and convicted, and were hanged on Gibbet Hill by the side of the Devil's Punchbowl. The site of the sailor's murder is now marked with an inscribed stone known as the Sailor's Stone. The sailor lies buried in Thursley churchyard, whilst the Red Lion Inn is now a private home.

The countryside around Hindhead and Thursley and into the Devil's Punchbowl was once the haunt of 'broom squires'. They eked out a living cutting birch trees and heather to make their besom broom handles and brushes, which were sold in country towns.

The 19th-century poet Alfred, Lord Tennyson loved Haslemere and the Surrey Hills. Aldworth, his former home, is in Lurgashall in Sussex, but close to Haslemere, along the now renamed Tennyson Lane. After Tennyson's death in 1892, Edward Burne-Jones designed a window in St Bartholomew's Church in Haslemere as a memorial to him.

The Dolmetsch family came to Haslemere in the 1920s and began their business manufacturing instruments of early music; it was the Dolmetsch family that instigated the revival of descant recorders, much used in primary schools. The annual International Dolmetsch Early Music Festival which is held every July was established by Arnold Dolmetsch in 1925 to perform early music in the town.

Did You Know?
SURREY
A MISCELLANY

The massed ranks of the staff pose outside Haslemere's post office around 1906 in photograph H35502 (below). At this time the post office would be providing three deliveries and seven collections on weekdays to residents, while the telegraph boys would also be on hand to deliver urgent telegrams.

From the 14th to the 17th centuries, Chiddingfold was the centre of a great glass-making industry with French, Flemish and German craftsmen coming there to work. The names of some of the foreign glassmakers, such as William le Franceis and John Alemayn, appear on a brass tablet in St Mary's Church, below a small window made of fragments of original old glass.

HASLEMERE, WEST STREET POST OFFICE c1906 H35502

CRANLEIGH, THE STATION 1908 59697

On the side of a pillar in the north transept of Cranleigh's medieval parish church of St Nicolas is a 12th-century carving known as the 'Cheshire Cat' which is reputed to have been Lewis Carroll's inspiration for the grinning cat character in his book 'Alice's Adventures in Wonderland'. Lewis Carroll's sisters lived in a house called The Chestnuts on Castle Hill at Guildford and he spent many holidays in the area, so may well have visited the church. Lewis Carroll died at The Chestnuts in Guildford in 1898 and is buried in Mount Cemetery in the town.

ABINGER HAMMER, THE CLOCK 1909 61362

On the road linking Guildford and Dorking, Abinger Hammer was one of the medieval centres of the local iron industry, and is named from the hammer-pond that worked a furnace there; the Tillingbourne was dammed to provide power for the mechanical hammers. The village's local landmark is the large clock that overhangs the A25, featuring a figure of Jack the Smith that strikes the bell every hour; local lore says that those who are present at midnight will see the figure change his grip on the hammer as the hour is struck.

The village of Westcott is famous for its unusual village sign, which also incorporates a thatched dovecote, signpost and direction indicator. It was erected on the village green as a First World War memorial. The weathervane has had the letter 'N' signifying north replaced by a 'T', so that is shows the letters W E S T, appropriate for Westcott.

Dorking was a major market town in the past. Cattle were brought into the town to be sold there, and would then be driven on to London, or over the Downs to Chatham through Sevenoaks. At one time so many sheep were sold at Dorking's market that pens stretched all along the north side of High Street. The view of the High Street in the early 1900s shown in photograph 53333 (below) has now changed out of all recognition – though the White Horse, a famous coaching inn on the right of the picture, still stands, and is said to be the oldest inn in the town. The ancient cellars of the inn are carved out of the sandstone on which Dorking stands, and from them a passage leads down to an old well. The inn building we see today dates from the 15th century, with the long street frontage probably built in the early 18th century.

In 1983 the claw of a dinosaur was discovered in the Smokejack clay pit near Dorking by William Walker. Further investigations revealed more fossilised remains of a previously unknown species of a fish-eating dinosaur, which had a long curved claw on each hand; it was named Baryonyx walkeri after the man who found it. The remains can now be seen at the Natural History Museum in London.

DORKING, HIGH STREET AND THE WHITE HORSE 1905 53333

MICKLEHAM, THE RUNNING HORSES INN 1897 39002

The Running Horses Inn at Mickleham is named after the Derby of 1828, in which 'The Colonel' and 'Cadland' ran a dead heat. The race had to be re-run and 'Cadland' was the eventual winner.

Surrey's famous beauty spot of Box Hill near Dorking derived its name from the box trees that used to grow there, many of which were cut down in the 18th and 19th centuries to make wood-engraving blocks. Box Hill features in Jane Austen's novel 'Emma', published in 1816, when some of the characters visit the beauty spot for a picnic: 'We are going to Box Hill tomorrow … It is not Switzerland but it will be something for a young man so much in want of change.' The characters were most enthusiastic when they reached their destination: 'Seven miles were travelled in expectation of enjoyment and everybody had a burst of admiration on arriving'. The Salomons Memorial on the summit of Box Hill commemorates Leopold Salomons of Norbury Park at Mickleham, who purchased much of Box Hill for the nation to enjoy and donated it to the National Trust in the early years of the 20th century.

A curiosity on Box Hill is the gravestone of Major Peter Labelliere, an eccentric resident of Dorking who was buried there in 1800. The Major asked in his will that the youngest son and daughter of his landlady 'will dance on my grave' – it is not known whether they fulfilled his request, but crowds of people attended his funeral, and for many years people would visit the Major's grave on the anniversary of his death and picnic and dance there in memory of him. His gravestone records that he was 'buried here head downwards' – see quiz question and answer number 4 to find out why.

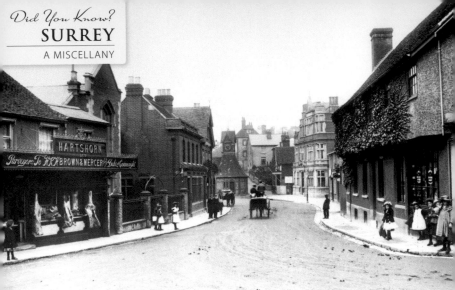

LEATHERHEAD, NORTH STREET 1906 54878

The name of Leatherhead is derived from the Saxon 'Leodridan', meaning 'public ford'; the town was a crossing place on the River Mole, and has remained a major road centre ever since. The quaint clock tower that used to stand at the foot of Gravel Hill, seen at the end of the street in photograph 54878 (above), was demolished during the redevelopment that has overtaken Leatherhead. In recent decades many historic buildings on the town's High Street have been lost, but one that remains is Cradlers House, a restored 14th-century hall house that is probably the oldest building in the town centre.

Samuel Pepys knew Ashtead, near Leatherhead, as a boy, and in later years called it 'my old place of delight'. After the First World War the Ashtead Pottery was set up to provide employment for ex-servicemen, and was in business in the village from 1923 to 1935. It produced a range of characteristic wares that are now very collectable.

The two boys in uniform standing with their bicycles outside Cobham post office in photograph 63129 (below) may well have been telegraph boys, ready to deliver a telegram. Not far from the village was an earlier form of communication – the semaphore tower on Telegraph Hill at Chatley Heath, which still survives. It was one of a series of 13 hilltop semaphore stations set up in the early 19th century by the Admiralty to send messages from London to the Fleet at Portsmouth. The towers used a system of articulated wooded 'arms' on the roofs, which were moved around in different combinations to form semaphore versions of letters of the alphabet and numbers.

COBHAM, THE POST OFFICE 1911 63129

Woking as we know it today grew up when the London to Southampton railway arrived in 1838, and is now one of Surrey's biggest towns. Woking has mushroomed in size and been redeveloped since it was first established in the 19th century, and few of the town's older Victorian buildings survive – the Old Bank on the corner of Chertsey Road, seen in photograph 46342 (below), for instance, had no place in the modernised Woking of the second half of the 20th century.

WOKING, THE OLD BANK 1901 46342

WOKING, THE SHAH JEHAN MOSQUE c1955 W122045

Oriental Road in Woking takes its name from the Oriental Institute that used to be sited there, founded by Dr Gottlieb Leitner in the 1880s. As a result of the Institute being based in Woking, the town boasts the first mosque to be built in Britain, erected in 1889 in Oriental Road so that Muslim students at the Institute could have a place to worship. After Dr Leitner died in 1899 the Oriental Institute was closed, and the mosque stood empty until 1912, when Khwaja Kamal ud Din, an Indian barrister, came to England as the first Muslim missionary. He chose Woking for his headquarters as it already had a mosque, and he reopened the building for worship. Today, the Maybury area of Woking is the centre of a large Muslim community that still worships at the mosque regularly.

**WEYBRIDGE, THE VIEW FROM THE LINCOLN ARMS HOTEL
1890** 23589

The confluence of the River Thames with the River Wey at Weybridge was important for the transport of goods to and from London from early times, but the improvement of the River Wey in 1653 increased the amount of traffic using the waterways, making it easier to transport agricultural goods, including grain, and associated commodities like timber, chalk and lime to London, as well as gunpowder, from the mills at Chilworth. By the end of the 19th century the Thames was also being used for pleasure and relaxation. The local regattas were major social events, and the availability of punts and skiffs, or larger launches for hire, created employment on the river banks for boatbuilders.

In the 1530s Henry VIII built a palace on the Oatlands estate near Weybridge. Oatlands Palace was demolished after the Civil War and in the early 18th century a mansion house, Oatlands House, was built on the site; this burned down in 1794 and the house was rebuilt in Gothic style, and is now the Oatlands Park Hotel. The tall monument that stands on Monument Green in Weybridge was erected in memory of Frederica, Duchess of York, who lived at Oatlands House for many years, and died in 1820. She was a popular local benefactress who supported and paid for the education of many children in the area.

Queen's Road in Weybridge was formerly called The Grange, but was renamed around the time of Queen Victoria's Diamond Jubilee in 1897. It was used by Queen Victoria when she travelled from Windsor to the 18th-century Palladian mansion of Claremont, at Esher, then the home of her son and daughter-in-law, the Duke and Duchess of Albany, but originally built in the 1770s for Lord Clive of India. The house at Claremont is now used as a school, but the grounds are open to the public.

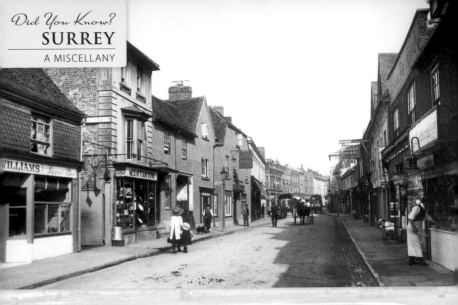

CHERTSEY, GUILDFORD STREET 1908 60929

Chertsey was once famed for its abbey, now almost entirely vanished. Nowadays it is famous for the story of Blanche Heriot, a heroine from the time of the Wars of the Roses. Her lover, a nephew of the Earl of Warwick, was captured by the Yorkists and was condemned to be executed in Chertsey when the curfew bell of St Peter's Church tolled. A messenger was sent to the king asking for a reprieve, but no reply had been received by the time the bell was due to ring, so Blanche climbed the church tower and hung on to the clapper of the bell so that it could not sound. The reprieve arrived an hour after the curfew should have been rung, and her lover's life was spared.

The Town Hall of Staines famously has a mistake on one of its clock faces. Amongst its Roman numerals, the XI is used twice, once as 11 and once as 9. (X1 is the correct form for 11, 9 should have been given as IX).

Staines originated as a military posting-station between the Roman towns of 'Londinium' (London) and 'Calleva Atrebatum' (Silchester), at the point where the Roman road crossed the Thames. The Roman engineers constructed several bridges to cross the multi-channelled River Thames here, and in their day the place was known as 'Ad Pontes', or 'Pontibu' – 'at the bridges'. Photograph 57990 (below) shows the graceful three-arched bridge over the Thames which was rebuilt in 1832 by John and George Rennie, close to the site of many bridges that have crossed the Thames since the Romans first spanned it.

Until the 14th century, the River Thames was tidal as far as Staines. Downstream from Staines the river was managed by the City of London, and a marker stone – the 'London Stone' – was set up in Staines in 1197 to indicate the westernmost limit of its jurisdiction. The London Stone originally stood beside the medieval bridge, but was moved to the area of Staines called The Lammas in 1832. The original London Stone is now in the Town Hall: the object currently at The Lammas is a replica.

STAINES, THE BRIDGE 1907 57990

WALTON-ON-THAMES, THE ANGLERS 1908   60037

The impressive Shannon Memorial in St Mary's Church at Walton-on-Thames commemorates Field Marshall Richard Boyle, the first Viscount Shannon, who lived at Ashley House and died in 1727 after an outstanding military career. It is one of the best works of Louis-François Roubiliac (or Roubillac), one of the foremost sculptors of the 18th century, and shows Viscount Shannon leaning on a mortar with a tent in the background. The church is also famous for the series of Selwyn Brasses, which commemorate John Selwyn, who was Gentleman Keeper of the Royal Park of Oatlands until his death in 1587. The first three brasses show John, his wife Susan and their 11 children. The fourth shows John mounted on a galloping stag with his hunting knife in the stag's neck. This is said to commemorate an incident which took place in the presence of Queen Elizabeth I, when the Keeper leaped from his horse and plunged his knife into the beast, so that it fell dead at the monarch's feet.

Until it was stolen in 1965, a scold's bridle dated 1633 was held in the vestry of St Mary's Church at Walton-on-Thames as a warning to brides who passed by on the way to their wedding. It came to the parish from Chester in 1793 and bore the following inscription:

Chester presents Walton with a bridle
To curb women's tongues that talk too idle.

A replica of the original is now held in a case by the north aisle of the church. It is a fearsome metallic object made to fit over the head with a bit clamping the tongue, thereby prohibiting speech, and would have been used on women accused of overly 'scolding' (nagging), gossiping or slanderous behaviour.

Epsom was recorded as 'Ebbisham' in the Domesday Book of 1086. The oldest part of the town grew up around the parish church of St Martin in what is now Church Street. The present chancel and transept of the church was rebuilt in 1907 in a hybrid Decorated Gothic cum Romanesque style. In 1856 Isabella Mayson married Samuel Beeton in St Martin's Church in Epsom, and went on to achieve fame as Mrs Beeton, author of the famous 'Book of Household Management'. Isabella's childhood home of Ormonde House at the east end of Epsom's High Street was replaced by a shopping parade in the 1890s.

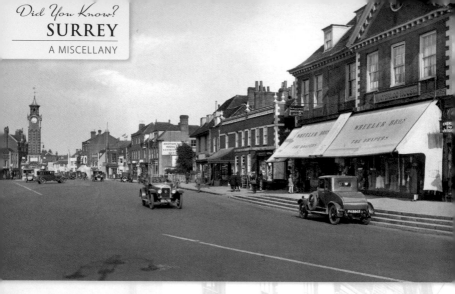

Did You Know?
SURREY
A MISCELLANY

EPSOM, HIGH STREET, WATERLOO HOUSE 1928 80803

Epsom developed in the 17th century as a spa town, when a mineral spring of water rich in magnesium and sulphates was discovered. The purgative efficacy of the unpleasant-tasting waters, a powerful antidote to constipation in those over-indulgent days, soon became well known and people flocked to the town. Entertainment facilities for the visitors developed, and by 1680 the New Tavern provided a tavern, coffee house and Assembly Rooms for public gatherings. The New Tavern and Assembly Rooms is the building shown on the right of photograph 80803 (above) in 1928, when it had become known as Waterloo House and been divided into shops. The building has now been restored to its original function and is a pub known as the Assembly Rooms.

The clock tower that is a landmark of Epsom's High Street was erected in 1847 to commemorate the passing of the Public Health Act.

Epsom declined as a spa after the 1720s, partly because chemists discovered how to replicate the therapeutic qualities of its spa water by boiling it down to make Epsom Salts, which then could be remixed with water and taken as a tonic or purgative. The mass production of Epsom Salts meant that that people could now purge themselves in the comfort of their own home. However, the town's other qualities attracted many rich Londoners who built themselves fine Georgian houses in the area, and Epsom evolved into a prosperous town. In 1962 Nikolaus Pevsner described Epsom as having more late Stuart, Queen Anne and Georgian houses than any other town in Surrey.

Epsom is famous for its racecourse on the Downs south of the town, the home of the Derby, probably the most famous flat horse race in Britain. A bronze sculpture in front of Epsom's Ebbisham Centre depicts two racehorses, captured at the moment of victory – Diomed, the winner of the first Derby in 1780, and Galileo, the winner of the 2001 Derby.

The Queen's Stand at the Epsom racecourse featured as the airport of St Petersburg in the James Bond film 'Goldeneye' (1995).

EPSOM, DERBY DAY 1928 81595

EWELL, HIGH STREET 1924 75489x

Ewell was once a Roman settlement on the Roman road now known as Stane Street, which crossed over Surrey and linked London to 'Noviomagus Regnensium', near modern Chichester. In later centuries the village developed beside the springs that feed the Hogsmill River, and parts of Ewell still retain 16th-century timber-framed and jettied houses. In Church Street is the old Watch House, a small late 18th-century building that is part village lock-up and part fire-engine shed – in those days the fire-engine was a small hand-hauled and hand-pumped contraption. The principal trade of Ewell in former times was gunpowder production, made in two mills in the village. In the 19th century Rectory Farm in Ewell, now demolished, belonged to the uncle of the Pre-Raphaelite artist William Holman Hunt, who often visited there. His picture of 1854, 'The Light of the World', was painted nearby, using a hut of one of the village gunpowder mills for the cottage at whose door Christ is shown.

At Lower Kingswood, south of Banstead, is a church that is unique in Britain. The Church of the Wisdom of God, at the junction of Brighton Road and Buckland Road, was built in the 1890s in the style of a Roman basilica, and some of the artefacts and marbles within it were salvaged from ancient Rome and Byzantium.

Caterham is in two parts, up the hill where the medieval church is, and Caterham Valley to the east on the valley floor, which grew up when the railway arrived in 1856. St Lawrence's Church in the old part of Caterham dates back to 1095-96 and was refashioned in the 13th century. An ancient face can be found looking across the chancel, hidden in the foliage of one of the capitals that has now been inserted into one of the walls, and a grinning head greets visitors in the nave arcade. Charles Asprey, the Bond Street jeweller, came to live at Caterham in the 1860s and became a great benefactor to the town. In photograph 78135 (below) we see the drinking fountain he donated in 1890 in its original position in Caterham, on what is now the roundabout in Station Avenue. It now stands in Church Walk.

CATERHAM, THE SQUARE 1925 78135

The original name for Reigate was 'Cherchefelle', meaning 'a place with a church in an open space', and this was the name recorded in the Domesday Book of 1086. By the end of the 12th century, 'Cherchefelle' had been replaced by 'Reigate', thought to refer to either the local 'reye', a word for roe deer, or Wray, a locality in the manor. After the Norman Conquest a castle was built at Reigate that has vanished completely, but its 11th-century motte is now a rose garden known as Castle Grounds.

Beneath Reigate are a number of caves that were used as shelters during the Second World War. The sand caves to the west of Tunnel Road were converted for public use as an air raid shelter and attracted people from as far away as London. The caves were cold, damp and smelly but for most people they were better than a night exposed to bombs. The east side of the caves, nearer to the Town Hall, were on stand-by for council staff in case of a daytime raid, but there were also 'rooms' put aside for the Bomb Report Centre and the headquarters of the police and fire brigade as well as a First Aid post. The Barons' Caves south of Tunnel Road were used as air raid shelters for pupils from local schools; on some occasions during the war, lessons were conducted down there.

**REIGATE
THE TOWN HALL
AND MARKET PLACE
1925** 78937

REDHILL, HIGH STREET 1906 55035

Dame Margot Fonteyn, Britain's greatest ballet dancer, was born in Reigate in 1919; her real name was Peggy Hookham. She became prima ballerina of the Vic-Wells Ballet, then formed ballet's most famous partnership with Rudolf Nureyev at the Royal Ballet in the 1960s and early 1970s. She is commemorated in Reigate by a statue in London Road.

Redhill, named from the sandstone hill south of the town centre, was called 'Redehelde' by the Saxons. In the 16th century it was 'Redd Hyll', and 100 years later it was 'Red Hill by Reigate'. For a time in the 19th century, as the new town sprang up, it was also known as 'Warwick Town'. It was only when the post office began franking letters from there with 'Redhill' that the name finally stuck. Redhill grew from nothing after the building of the London to Brighton road c1818 and the coming of the railway c1840, when the London and Brighton Railway (LBR) opened Red Hill and Reigate Road Station (as it was then called) to serve Reigate, two miles to the west.

The artist John Linnell (1792-1882) was changing trains in Redhill in 1849 when he saw the potential for landscape painting in the area. He built a house and studio on Redstone Hill and painted many pictures of Redstone Wood and Redstone Hollow. One of the better known, Noon Day Rest, is in the Tate Gallery.

One of England's greatest astronomers built his own observatory in Redhill and made observations there that won him international acclaim and The Royal Astronomical Society's Gold Medal. Richard Carrington built his house and observatory in Furze Hill in 1852 where he compiled a catalogue of 3,785 circumpolar stars, and then did original work on sunspots and solar flares which he connected with geomagnetic storms. The site of his house is now part of a housing estate, but he is commemorated in the names of Carrington Close and Dome Way. The Sun pub in London Road in Redhill was also named in memory of Richard Carrington, whose work determined elements of the rotation axis of the sun.

Photograph 63427 (opposite) shows employees leaving the Monotype works at Salfords in 1911. Note how smartly dressed they all are, all wearing a tie and cap. Monotype came to Salfords in 1901, and made hot metal castings for the printing trade. Monotype is still in the area; it now operates in the modern computer age, and is part of the AGFA group.

The first railway to be built in Surrey was the Surrey Iron Railway (SIR), which was also the first public railway in the world, although no passengers ever travelled on it. It was a horse-drawn system, built before locomotives were viable. The first 8½-mile Wandsworth-Croydon section was opened in 1802 and the second Croydon-Merstham section of 10 miles in 1805. The railway was used to carry stone and lime from quarries around Merstham. By the time it closed in 1839, it was also carrying 6,000 tons of fuller's earth each year. The slow SIR lost out to steam and sold its land to the LBRC for the London-Brighton railway line. Little of the SLR remains in the area, but in the Memorial Gardens at Quality Street in Merstham are the remains of four tracks used for the line.

SALFORDS, THE MONOTYPE WORKS 1911 63427

HORLEY, THE SIX BELLS 1906 55378

Horley was just a series of hamlets on the London to Brighton road until the area began to be developed after the railway arrived in 1841. The historic Six Bells Inn (15th-century with later additions and a Horsham stone roof) was an old coaching inn on the main road. Close by is the parish church of St Bartholomew. Inside the church, on the north wall of the chancel, is a particularly fine memorial brass, dating from about 1420, which depicts a medieval lady in an elegant gown with long flowing sleeves, and wearing a stylish horned head-dress.

Horley is home to a most unusual theatre – the Archway Theatre is located underneath the arches of the Victoria Road railway bridge and is the only 'under the arches' theatre in the country. The main auditorium seats 95 people, and 10 full productions are staged each year by the Archway Theatre Company, as well as a number of other events.

Photograph 54733 (below) shows the two mills which used to stand at Outwood. The smock mill on the right, so called because of its resemblance to a countryman's working garment, no longer stands. The post mill on the left is still there. It was built in the 17th century and has since been restored, and is the oldest working windmill in Britain.

In the 18th century, water that reputedly cured gout was being drawn from a well in Godstone that had been sunk beside a pear tree. No one could eat the fruit of the tree as it was so hard – but the Iron Peartree Water was much sought after, and could be bought at the White Hart Inn in the village for a shilling a bottle. People came from miles around to take the cure.

OUTWOOD, THE WINDMILLS 1906 54733

Photograph 52989 (below) shows the landmark building in the centre of Lingfield, known as the Old Cage, which used to serve as the village lock up, or prison; it was last used in 1882. Lingfield's 14th-century parish church of St Peter and St Paul contains a fascinating series of brass effigies on the tombs of the first three Baron Cobhams. These show the development of a knight's armour over the period between the death of the 1st Baron in 1361 and the 3rd Baron in 1446.

LINGFIELD, THE OLD CAGE AND THE POND 1904 52989

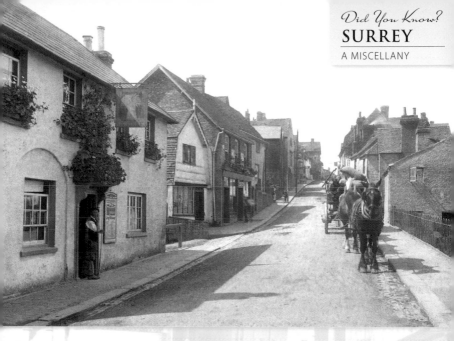

OXTED, THE VILLAGE 1906 54251

The name of Oxted derived from 'Ac stede', meaning 'the place of oak trees'. The oldest church in Oxted is St Mary's, which dates from Norman times and was originally built away from the medieval village, but is now surrounded by the modern town. Oxted is famous for its brass band, and also for its annual pram race event, which raises funds for charity. Participants in fancy dress have to push a pram from Master Park to the Bell in Old Oxted High Street, stopping at seven licensed establishments along the route where they have to down a drink as fast as possible before continuing.

SPORTING SURREY

Photograph 57883 (opposite) shows a scene at the Hindhead Golf Club in 1907, just three years after the Club had been founded. Sir Arthur Conan Doyle, creator of Sherlock Holmes, lived locally and was President of the Club from 1905 to 1907.

The first documented use of the word 'cricket' in the English language related to the games of children in the north ditch of Guildford. It was recorded during the course of an enquiry in 1598, when a John Derrick remembered that 'he did runne and play there at creckett and other plaies'. A famous name in Surrey's sporting history is that of the renowned cricketer William 'Silver Billy' Beldham, whose exploits made him the greatest player of the late 18th and early 19th centuries. He was born at Wrecclesham in 1766 and played in Farnham Cricket Club's first match, when he was 16 years old; he later played for the famous Hambledon Club, and by the age of 21 he was widely considered to be the best batsman in England. A renowned cricketer from Dorking was Henry Jupp, born in the town in 1841. He had a very successful career as a batsman with Surrey, playing 378 games. Jupp became well known for an incident whilst playing in a match in his home town. He was bowled out by the first ball of the match, but just replaced the bails and stood his ground. On being asked by the umpires why he wasn't leaving the pitch, he famously replied 'Not at Dorking I ain't!'.

Mike Hawthorn Drive in Farnham, off Dogflud Way, is named after the racing driver Mike Hawthorn (1929-1959), who became the first British Formula One World Champion in 1958, driving for Ferrari. His family moved to Farnham from Mexborough in South Yorkshire when he was a small child and he lived there until his death in 1959, when he was killed in a road accident on the A31.

The famous National Rifle Association target-shooting range is at Bisley, where the annual world championship shooting competitions are held. The ranges run south-east to west, with the targets below the number boards on the bund, or earthwork, behind them.

A famous sportsman from Frimley is Jonny Wilkinson, a member of England's Rugby Union World Cup-winning team of 2003. He was born in Frimley in 1979 and began his rugby career playing for the minis team of Farnham Rugby Club.

Epsom is famous for two of England's five Classic flat horse races that are run on the Downs south of the town, the Derby and the Oaks. Horse racing is believed to have first taken place on Epsom Downs during the reign of James I, as a diversion for the king when he was staying at Nonsuch Palace nearby. By the 18th century racing was well established in the area, and the Oaks Stakes was first run in 1779 and the famous Derby in 1780. The Derby is contested by three-year-old colts and fillies, whilst only three-year-old fillies run in the Oaks Stakes over the same distance, 1 mile, 4 furlongs and 10 yards (2,423 metres). The Derby is the second leg of the English Triple Crown. It is preceded by the 2,000 Guineas, and followed by the St Leger.

HINDHEAD, THE GOLF HOUSE 1907 57883

QUIZ QUESTIONS

Answers on page 54.

1. According to tradition, how did the River Mole in Surrey get its name?

2. Woking is famous as the home of the McLaren Group, which produces Formula One racing cars from its huge Technology Centre in Chertsey Road, giving Surrey a local F1 team. But which famous racing cars used to be made in the Staines/Egham area?

3. How did the Derby horse race at Epsom get its name?

4. Leith Hill near Dorking is the highest point in south-east England. The tower on its summit was built by Richard Hull, the squire of Leith Hill Place, in 1766. After his death in 1772, Squire Hull was buried beneath the tower in an unusual way – what was it?

5. What is the connection between Leatherhead and the feature film 'Shakespeare in Love' of 1998?

6. Woking was destroyed by alien invaders in which famous science fiction book?

7. What place in motoring history is held by Mr John Henry Knight of Farnham?

8. The nickname of Dorking Football Club is 'The Chicks'. Why?

9. Why is Runnymede, the stretch of water meadow beside the River Thames near Egham in Surrey, a famous name in English history?

10. For many centuries an important industry in Surrey has been the extraction and production of the county's rich deposits of fuller's earth, dug from quarries such as those around Redstone Hill, east of Redhill. The fuller's earth produced in Surrey is regarded as the best of its kind in the country, and is the county's best natural resource. What is fuller's earth, and what is it used for?

Did You Know?
SURREY
A MISCELLANY

RECIPE

SURREY CHURDLES

Churdles are savoury snacks made with lambs' liver, which were popular in both Surrey and Sussex in the past.

225g/8oz shortcrust pastry
1 tablespoonful browned breadcrumbs
A small amount of grated cheese
Bacon fat or vegetable oil for frying
1 large sliced onion
225g/8oz sliced lambs' liver
225g/8oz chopped bacon rashers or pieces, with the rind taken off
50g/2oz chopped mushrooms
1 medium cooking apple, peeled, cored and chopped
1 tablespoonful chopped parsley
1 teaspoonful dried rosemary
Salt and pepper to taste
Beaten egg, to glaze

Pre-heat the oven to 180°C/350°F/Gas Mark 4.

Fry the onion, liver and bacon in the fat or oil until nicely browned. Mince or finely chop together the cooked onion, liver and bacon, then add the mushrooms, apple, parsley, rosemary and salt and pepper, and mix well.

Roll out the pastry and cut out 15cm (6 inch) rounds. Divide the liver mixture between the rounds, then shape the pastry dough up around it to form a pasty shape, but leaving the mixture exposed in the centre. Mix together the breadcrumbs and cheese and sprinkle over the exposed centres. Place the Churdles on a baking sheet and brush with beaten egg. Bake in the pre-heated oven for about 30 minutes, until the pastry is golden. These are delicious served with redcurrant jelly.

SUNBURY-ON-THAMES, THE MAGPIE HOTEL 1890 23560

EAST MOLESEY, STEAMBOATS ON THE LOCK 1896 38350x

RECIPE

DEVILLED CHICKEN LEGS

A traditional name for people from Surrey in the past was a 'Surrey Capon', as the county was renowned as a place where chickens were fattened up for the London markets. (A 'capon' is a cockerel that has been castrated, producing a bird with more tender meat). 'Devilling', or adding a mustard sauce to food, was very popular in Victorian and Edwardian times. This fiery, spicy dish could either be eaten hot with strips of buttered toast, or taken on picnics or boating trips to be eaten cold.

  2 teaspoonfuls English mustard powder
  1 teaspoonful salt
  Half a teaspoonful freshly ground black pepper
  Half a teaspoonful cayenne pepper
  Half a teaspoonful paprika
  2 teaspoonfuls mild curry powder
  3 teaspoonfuls French mustard
  50g (2oz) butter
  8 cooked chicken legs
  1 tablespoonful plain flour

Mix the mustard powder with half the salt, pepper, cayenne and paprika, the curry powder and the French mustard and work to a paste. Add half the butter and work again to a paste. Make 4 slits down the length of each chicken leg and spread a little of the devil mixture in each. Season the flour with the remaining salt, pepper, cayenne and paprika, and use it to dust the chicken legs. Melt the remaining butter and brush it over each leg.

Place the chicken legs under a pre-heated hot grill and cook for about 5 minutes, turning to brown the legs on all sides. Baste with the grill pan juices once or twice during cooking.

QUIZ ANSWERS

1. The River Mole is so named because it disappears beneath Box Hill, near Dorking, into the subterranean clefts in the chalk, only to reappear again, like a mole, near Leatherhead.

2. Lagondas. The Lagonda car firm began in a back garden in Thorpe Road, Staines in 1906 when the householder, Wilbur Gunn, made his first car. He was an Ohio man from the USA, and took the name Lagonda from a river near his hometown. For many years Lagonda cars were produced at a large factory at Egham Hythe, where Sainsbury's now stands, but the Lagonda company was purchased and integrated into Aston Martin in 1947 and left the area.

3. The Derby horse race got its name from the 12th Earl of Derby, who suggested to his friend Sir Charles Bunbury that they should fund a new short and exciting race for three-year-old horses. They decided to run the first race at Epsom Downs in 1780. They tossed a coin to decide which of them would give it a name, and it is by pure chance that the race is not now famous throughout the world as the Bunbury.

4. Richard Hull was buried head downwards beneath the tower after his death in 1772, in accordance with an interpretation, prevalent at the time, of the biblical reference regarding the Day of Judgement when the world will be turned upside down and the dead resurrected. Squire Hill anticipated being amongst the few souls who would then face their Creator the right way up. A gravestone on Box Hill near Dorking marks the resting place of Major Peter Labelliere, who was buried head downwards there for the same reason.

5. The Edmund Tylney pub in Leatherhead is named after an important local resident in the past who lived in the Mansion House. Sir Edmund Tylney (c1536-1610) was Queen Elizabeth I's Master of the Revels, the Elizabethan version of today's official censor, and one of his tasks was to read and approve William Shakespeare's plays for public performance. Sir Edmund Tylney featured as a character in the film 'Shakespeare in Love', where he was played by Simon Callow.

6. 'The War of the Worlds' by H G Wells, who was living in Maybury Road in Woking when he wrote his famous book. Published in 1898, it dealt with a Martian invasion of Woking, culminating in the destruction of the town. To celebrate the centenary of the book's publication, in 1998 a stainless steel structure of a Martian tripod entitled 'The Martian Landing' was installed in Crown Passage in Woking.

7. Mr John Henry Knight of Farnham, a wealthy engineer and inventor, is credited with building the first petrol-powered motor car ever to be driven on British roads in premises on West Street in the town in 1895, with the assistance of engineer George Parfitt. He proudly drove his three-wheeled vehicle through the town on 17th October 1895, but was fined five shillings for not having a traction engine licence, nor a man walking in front with a red flag to warn people of the danger approaching.

8. The nickname of Dorking Football Club of 'The Chicks' is a reference to the Dorking Fowl, a breed of chicken that takes its name from the town and was once extensively bred there. A peculiar and unique characteristic of the Dorking Fowl breed is that it possesses a fifth claw.

9. It was at Runnymede that in 1215 a group of barons persuaded King John to affix his seal to the Magna Carta, the 'great charter of liberties'. The reason for its symbolic importance in history are the clauses which declare 'No freeman shall be arrested or imprisoned or disseized or outlawed or exiled…except by the lawful judgement of his peers and by the law of the land', and 'To none will we sell, to none will we refuse or delay right or justice'. The Stephan Langton Inn in Friday Street in Surrey is named after the Archbishop of Canterbury who was born in the village; it was Archbishop Langton who drafted the Magna Carta and was a key figure in compelling King John to agree to it.

10. Fuller's earth is a non-plastic clay that has been used for centuries in the cleaning and preparation of woollen and worsted cloth. Fuller's earth is now also used in oil refining, a range of engineering applications, in the pharmaceutical industry and for cats' litter.

FRANCIS FRITH

PIONEER VICTORIAN PHOTOGRAPHER

Francis Frith, founder of the world-famous photographic archive, was a complex and multi-talented man. A devout Quaker and a highly successful Victorian businessman, he was philosophical by nature and pioneering in outlook. By 1855 he had already established a wholesale grocery business in Liverpool, and sold it for the astonishing sum of £200,000, which is the equivalent today of over £15,000,000. Now in his thirties, and captivated by the new science of photography, Frith set out on a series of pioneering journeys up the Nile and to the Near East.

INTRIGUE AND EXPLORATION

He was the first photographer to venture beyond the sixth cataract of the Nile. Africa was still the mysterious 'Dark Continent', and Stanley and Livingstone's historic meeting was a decade into the future. The conditions for picture taking confound belief. He laboured for hours in his wicker dark-room in the sweltering heat of the desert, while the volatile chemicals fizzed dangerously in their trays. Back in London he exhibited his photographs and was 'rapturously cheered' by members of the Royal Society. His reputation as a photographer was made overnight.

VENTURE OF A LIFE-TIME

By the 1870s the railways had threaded their way across the country, and Bank Holidays and half-day Saturdays had been made obligatory by Act of Parliament. All of a sudden the working man and his family were able to enjoy days out, take holidays, and see a little more of the world.

With typical business acumen, Francis Frith foresaw that these new tourists would enjoy having souvenirs to commemorate their days out. For the next thirty years he travelled the country by train and by pony and trap, producing fine photographs of seaside resorts and beauty spots that were keenly bought by millions of Victorians. These prints were painstakingly pasted into family albums and pored over during the dark nights of winter, rekindling precious memories of summer excursions. Frith's studio was soon supplying retail shops all over the country, and by 1890 F Frith & Co had become the greatest specialist photographic publishing company in the world, with over 2,000 sales outlets, and pioneered the picture postcard.

FRANCIS FRITH'S LEGACY

Francis Frith had died in 1898 at his villa in Cannes, his great project still growing. By 1970 the archive he created contained over a third of a million pictures showing 7,000 British towns and villages.

Frith's legacy to us today is of immense significance and value, for the magnificent archive of evocative photographs he created provides a unique record of change in the cities, towns and villages throughout Britain over a century and more. Frith and his fellow studio photographers revisited locations many times down the years to update their views, compiling for us an enthralling and colourful pageant of British life and character.

We are fortunate that Frith was dedicated to recording the minutiae of everyday life. For it is this sheer wealth of visual data, the painstaking chronicle of changes in dress, transport, street layouts, buildings, housing and landscape that captivates us so much today, offering us a powerful link with the past and with the lives of our ancestors.

Computers have now made it possible for Frith's many thousands of images to be accessed almost instantly. The archive offers every one of us an opportunity to examine the places where we and our families have lived and worked down the years. Its images, depicting our shared past, are now bringing pleasure and enlightenment to millions around the world a century and more after his death.

For further information visit: www.francisfrith.com

INTERIOR DECORATION

Frith's photographs can be seen framed and as giant wall murals in thousands of pubs, restaurants, hotels, banks, retail stores and other public buildings throughout Britain. These provide interesting and attractive décor, generating strong local interest and acting as a powerful reminder of gentler days in our increasingly busy and frenetic world.

FRITH PRODUCTS

All Frith photographs are available as prints and posters in a variety of different sizes and styles. In the UK we also offer a range of other gift and stationery products illustrated with Frith photographs, although many of these are not available for delivery outside the UK – see our web site for more information on the products available for delivery in your country.

THE INTERNET

Over 100,000 photographs of Britain can be viewed and purchased on the Frith web site. The web site also includes memories and reminiscences contributed by our customers, who have personal knowledge of localities and of the people and properties depicted in Frith photographs. If you wish to learn more about a specific town or village you may find these reminiscences fascinating to browse. Why not add your own comments if you think they would be of interest to others? See **www.francisfrith.com**

PLEASE HELP US BRING FRITH'S PHOTOGRAPHS TO LIFE

Our authors do their best to recount the history of the places they write about. They give insights into how particular towns and villages developed, they describe the architecture of streets and buildings, and they discuss the lives of famous people who lived there. But however knowledgeable our authors are, the story they tell is necessarily incomplete.